How to Eradicate Fear

A Guide for Entrepreneurs

By Nicole Lee

Copyright © 2020 Nicole Lee

"How to Eradicate Fear- A Guide for Entrepreneurs" is created to stimulate a new thought and awareness in your Consciousness while along your spiritual journey. All rights reserved. This book is protected under the copyright laws of the United States of America and Spiritual laws of the Universe. No part of this book may be copied, reprinted, reproduced, stored in a retrieval system, transmitted, reproduced by any mechanical, photographic or electronic process or in any form of recording; nor may it be stored in a retrieval system, transmitted or otherwise be copied for public or private use other than for fair use as a brief quotation embodied in articles and reviews, without obtaining prior written permission.

Dedication

"This book is dedicated, first to the Divine God Intelligence of the Universe, the source who created me, and the one who continues to guide me along this journey. I praise and honor the Almighty Divine God Intelligence! To my God-given gifts, my children: Darius, Dejah and Devin – I love you always- you are my reason for being and my inspiration of why I do what I do! Thank you for keeping me grounded."

~Nicole Lee

Introduction

We currently live in a society where people live in fear every day of their lives due to the pandemic, unemployment, and the uncertainties of our future. People's hopes, dreams, desires and aspirations have been covered by the smog of fear, depression, and negative influences of this world. By creating a space of authenticity and transparency without judgment creates a mindset of hope and ignites the idea of a bright future.

Entrepreneurship is purpose work and in order to press forward, having a positive mindset is key.

In this book, I will share and offer tools to use to overcome the negative emotions that seem to manifest overtime during an entrepreneur's life journey. This is one key component that keeps one from living a purposeful life.

This book is a guide and a tool to use and memorize positive affirmations when a negative emotion arises.

While reading this book, if you experience the specific emotion, repeat the remedy out loud until the emotion disappears.

Repetition creates habits within the mind and spirit. Overtime, you will master how to eliminate negative emotions and thoughts.

When one is in control of their emotions it no longer controls you, which ignites your mind towards great insights for your goals and aspirations in life.

Testimony

"Thank you, Nicole for an amazing lesson.

I'm so glad that I attended this class., "How to Eradicate Fear- A Guide for Entrepreneurs". I am mustering up all of my confidence, trust, and gumption to take full advantage of the opportunities :).

Also excited to stretch into these new abundance affirmations. I could honestly go on and on about all I got out of the class.

You are so nurturing and empowering and powerful and kind :) and I'm grateful for your guidance and for our connection." ~Jenna B.

Foreword

"Fear, doubt, procrastination, worry, criticism and indecisiveness are closely related, where one is found the others are nearby in thought and action. Fear paralyzes reasoning, accurate thinking, imagination, self-reliance, enthusiasm and initiative, it encourages uncertainty and procrastination. Fear comes in the form of being bound or whipped spiritually and physically.

A state of mind is something that you assume, it cannot be purchased, it must be created. The subconscious mind accepts the dominant ideas, mood or feelings one has. Choosing ideas, mood or feelings of positivity will rule the subconscious mind and your actions will mimic."

Fear is as powerful as Faith

Which one will you choose to guide your life?

The emotions of fear and faith have equal pulling power,

one attracts failure,

the other attracts greatness,

Which one will you choose?

FEAR?

"SPEAK OUT-LOUD THE 37TH PSALM TO CLEANSE YOUR ATMOSPHERE AND FEAR FROM WITHIN"

"Fear"

"1 Do not fret because of those who are evil or be envious of those who do wrong; 2 for like the grass they will soon wither, like green plants they will soon die away. 3 Trust in the Trust in the LORD and do good; dwell in the land and enjoy safe pasture. 4 Take delight in the Take delight in the LORD, and he will give you the desires of your heart. 5 Commit your way to the LORD; trust in him and he will do this: 6 He will make your righteous reward shine like the dawn, your vindication like the noonday sun. 7 Be still before the LORD and wait patiently for him; do not fret when people succeed in their ways when they carry out their wicked schemes. 8 Refrain from anger and turn from wrath; do not fret—it leads only to evil.
9 For those who are evil will be destroyed, but those who hope in the LORD will inherit the land." ~ Psalms 37:1-9

Positive Affirmations

- We are the source of all wealth. We are rich with creative ideas. Our mind abounds with new, original, inspired thoughts. What we have to offer is unique, and the world desires it. Our value is beyond reckoning. What the world needs and desires, we recognize and fulfill. The bounty of our mind is without hindrance or limit. Nothing can stand in the way of our inspired creativeness"! Ase! (and so it is)

- How to activate this affirmation: Speak out loud this truth about self 3x daily. The affirmation will sink into the subconscious mind, where it begins the manifestation in physical form.

What is the Shift? The shift is an awakening to our true identity. It is the light being switched on in each and every one of us to the conscious understanding of who and what we truly are. Part of the knowledge received is that we are a Soul having Human experiences. We inhabit a body, but this body is not who and what we are; it is a vehicle that we have been given to have mobility and experience on this physical plane of existence. How can this transition be more knowledgeable, have a simpler understanding? How can we, as awakened beings, fear less? How can it be a bit smoother, more inviting, and more acceptable to those being affected by the shift?

This is how: "Begin to erase FEAR from the mind."

How? Erase fear from the mind by allowing the DIVINE GOD INTELLIGENCE to take complete control of your life.

While allowing God to do such work for you, what is the price, you ask??

Obedience to whatever God instructs you to do. Obedience is better than Sacrifice.

FEAR=False Evidence Appearing Real.

God is not the Spirit of fear.

Knowing God's voice (positive thoughts that are for your own good), getting quiet through daily meditation and surrounding yourself around POSITIVE people is the beginning of igniting "On Earth as it is in Heaven" experience.

Thoughts?

Faith vs Fear

Think what you desire not what you "don't" want or think what "may" happen.

Faith is as powerful as Fear, which one will you choose to guide your life?

The emotions of fear attract failure and faith attracts greatness.

What is Faith? In my experience, faith is a supernatural reassured truth from within beyond thought.

What is Fear? False evidence appearing real in thought.

Repetition creates habit within the mind and spirit.

Overtime, you will master how to eliminate negative emotions and thoughts by practicing effective tools that work for you as an individual spirit.

WHAT YOU THINK WILL MANIFEST!

Thoughts?

Without a purpose, people perish..

Ask yourself these 3 questions and write it down:

- Why do I exist?

- What do I have to offer?

- Whom should I serve and why?

Answering these questions will ignite a desire from within that will trigger ideas of your purpose in life.

Two main fear entrepreneurs face:

- **Fear of success** is when you have an ongoing **fear of succeeding**, so much so that you might be inadvertently self-sabotaging. It's more about the **fear** to change and outside of your comfort zone.

- **Fear of failure** is when we allow that **fear** to stop you doing the things that can move us forward to achieve our goals.

Do you have any fears as an entrepreneur?

Why Business Fail?

- Lack of legal business forms, i.e. Business Plans, LLC

- Lack business etiquette, i.e., no call backs or email responses.

- Insufficient planning and research to find if business is profitable

- Inadequate start-up capital

- Failure to seek professional advice

- Insufficient expertise in the product or service

- Lack of marketing skills

- Lack online presence; i.e website, social media platforms, blog, etc.

Mission Statement

Now's the time to begin thinking about your mission statement for your business. Having a mission statement shows the reason for being and is the foundation of your business, your mission will transfer your passion into success.

Here's a tip:

A Mission Statement is how you move towards the vision of your business and what motivates and inspires you to pursue your vision.

Do you have a Mission Statement?

Write it here:

UNCERTAIN?

"ASK YOURSELF

WHY DO I EXIST?

WHAT DO I HAVE TO OFFER?

FINDING PURPOSE IN LIFE MAKES LIFE CERTAIN"

"Uncertainty"

"The cause of uncertainty is the uncertainty of your God-given PURPOSE in life.

Ask yourself these 3 questions:

Why do I exist?

What do I have to offer?

Whom should I serve and why?

Answering these questions will ignite a desire from within that will trigger ideas of a purposeful life."

Business Plan

As an entrepreneur, having a Business Plan is essential and will become a road map for your journey.

Having a business plan can ignite and change your uncertainty to being certain about your future and your business. With a plan, you can't be distracted by the forces of what life brings.

The business plan is just that – a PLAN – for a for profit, non-profit, product, service, or retail.

Consider it to be a map, something that guides your path and tracks your successes and failures.

"Without a plan, people become easily distracted…"

Here's a few simple questions to begin the process of writing your business plan:

1. What type of business are you creating?

2. What products or services will you sell?

3. Who will be your target audience?

4. How is it unique?

5. Who is your competitor?

6. How will you market your business?

7. How will you fund your start-up cost?

Thoughts?

"Anger"

"Channel the energy to something productive and creative. Write down the who, why and what is making you angry. Seek solutions to keep that emotion from returning. Practice forgiveness, this will eliminate any lingering anger from within that's blocking your decision to being happy. Let it go!"

"Loneliness"

"Loneliness comes from being alone which is a sign of the disconnection of your truest self and the highest energy source- God. Surround yourself with loving family and friends. Volunteering your time and energy to help someone in need will fill the void of loneliness and ignite the desire of your life's purpose.

Energy

"The vibration of fear passes from one mind to another just as quickly as the sound of one's voice. The person who gives expression, by word of mouth to negative or destructive thoughts, is certain to experience the action of negativity." ~ "Think and Grow Rich" by Napoleon Hill

There are six (6) senses of the human species; see, hear, taste, touch, smell, and 3rd Eye (spiritual intuition). Your senses will become more sensitive and heightened, to where you become more aware of the energies that surround you.
Because you have controlled your space of clearance of
any negative residue, it allows you to become "aware" when the vibrational frequency has changed…positive vs negative.

Any external source of negative energy can cause you to feel depressed, angry or fearful.

Energies are very easy to pick up from anyone or from anywhere. They can latch onto you when you've allowed yourself to be vulnerable.

When we are feeling low, our vibrations are easy targets for negative forces.

When we are happy, our vibrations are at a higher realm thereby making them an easy target for positive forces.

Thoughts?

White Sage

What is White SAGE?
It's a dried plant/herb, and when burned, it is utilized to rid a space of negative energies/spirits. When you have many different people/spirits dwelling under one space, this creates a lingering of energies, either positive/negative. This is why it is important to keep a positive conversation within your *Space*. People leave residues of their own energies behind. Burn sage in every room for the clearing of these lingering energies/spirits. This practice will make you more aware of the type of energies that come into your *Space*.

Frankincense Oil/Incense:

What is Frankincense oil/incense? It's an aroma worn on the skin as a covering or burned in the atmosphere to clear negative energies.

Hyssop Herb:

What is Hyssop? It's an herb used for tea (helps with anxiety). This herb is symbolized as a common cleansing in the Old Testament of the Bible; "Cleanse me with hyssop, and I will be clean"

Psalm 51:7

Thoughts?

Positive Thoughts

- Positive thoughts create positive outcomes by having a positive mental attitude. Love, Joy and Peace are thoughts of good energy.

- Negative thoughts create negative outcomes by having negative attitudes. Fear, Hate and Worry are thoughts of negative energy.

- It is healthy to talk to yourself. Tell yourself to stop when a negative thought enters your mind. Replace that thought with one that is positive.

- Avoid people who have what you do not want: a negative mental attitude.

"Restlessness"

"Guided Visual Meditation creates visions of peace that guide you towards a quiet, restful place in mind. Close your eyes. Think of a place you would like to travel to.
What will you take on this trip? Who will you want to go with? How will you get there? Create a picture in mind- in color, as you begin this journey."

Thoughts?

Affirmations

Here's a daily affirmation to speak to assist with embodying a positive mind and spirit.

"I dwell in the atmosphere of the Divine Intelligence God. I am thankful for all the blessings seen and unseen. I attract the energy of Love. I attract the energy of Joy. I attract the energy of Prosperity and Abundance. I am rich with creative ideas. My opportunities are expanded in such a way, so that I can be a vessel for God globally. What I have to offer to the world is greatly desired with great reward. My Vision and Faith manifest my heart's desires. And because I am aligned with the Divine God Intelligence, I am of Greatness!!

And in Full Faith I Consciously,Subconsciously and Superconsciously accept THIS manifest! Ase!

How to activate this affirmation:

Speak out loud this truth about yourself daily. The affirmation will sink into the subconscious mind, where it begins the manifestation in physical form.

Now write your own affirmation!

Tools

- Guided Visual Meditation creates visions of peace that guide you towards a quiet, restful place in mind.

- Fasting: Choose one of the things that you enjoy (food, TV or social media) and do without for 30 days.

- Naps: Take 20 minute naps or pauses of quietness daily, it resets the energy level and cells within the body.

- Turn the TV off: Your space must be free of any distraction of sound (TV, people), light a lavender candle, white sage, or frankincense incense.

- Breathe: Begin to inhale for 3 counts, exhale for 6 counts. Continue this until you feel relaxed and all thoughts in your mind are silent. Breathing brings forth oxygen to the brain. Oxygen is vital for brain healing and its proper function.

- Walk barefoot in the grass.

- Journal

- Pray

- Drink vegetable and fruit Smoothies.

- Laugh often.

- Spend less time on the internet.

- Light a lavender candle.

- Live life instead of just existing.

- Seek joy daily.

- Create a vision board.

- Meditate.

- Everything in moderation.

- Practice spiritual cleansing.

- Dismiss negative people.

- Exercise.
- Love yourself.

"Drained"

"Fasting: Choose one of the things that you enjoy (food, TV or social media) and do without for 30 days (it takes 30 days to create a habit). This will ignite discipline with self and creates awareness of who and what is draining you.

Naps: Take 30 minute naps or pauses of quietness daily, it resets the energy level and cells within the body."

"Unhappiness"

"Seek and connect with people who truly love you and desire greatness for your life. Speak Positive Affirmations daily, it'll jumpstart your day, your mind, your body and your spirit with joy and happiness!

"Stress"

"Your space must be free of any distraction of sound (TV, radio, people). Sit up straight or lay on your back. Choose tools of your choice to assist with relaxation: light a lavender candle, white sage, or frankincense incense. Close your eyes. Begin to inhale for 3 counts, exhale for 6 counts. Continue this until you feel relaxed and all thoughts in your mind are silent."

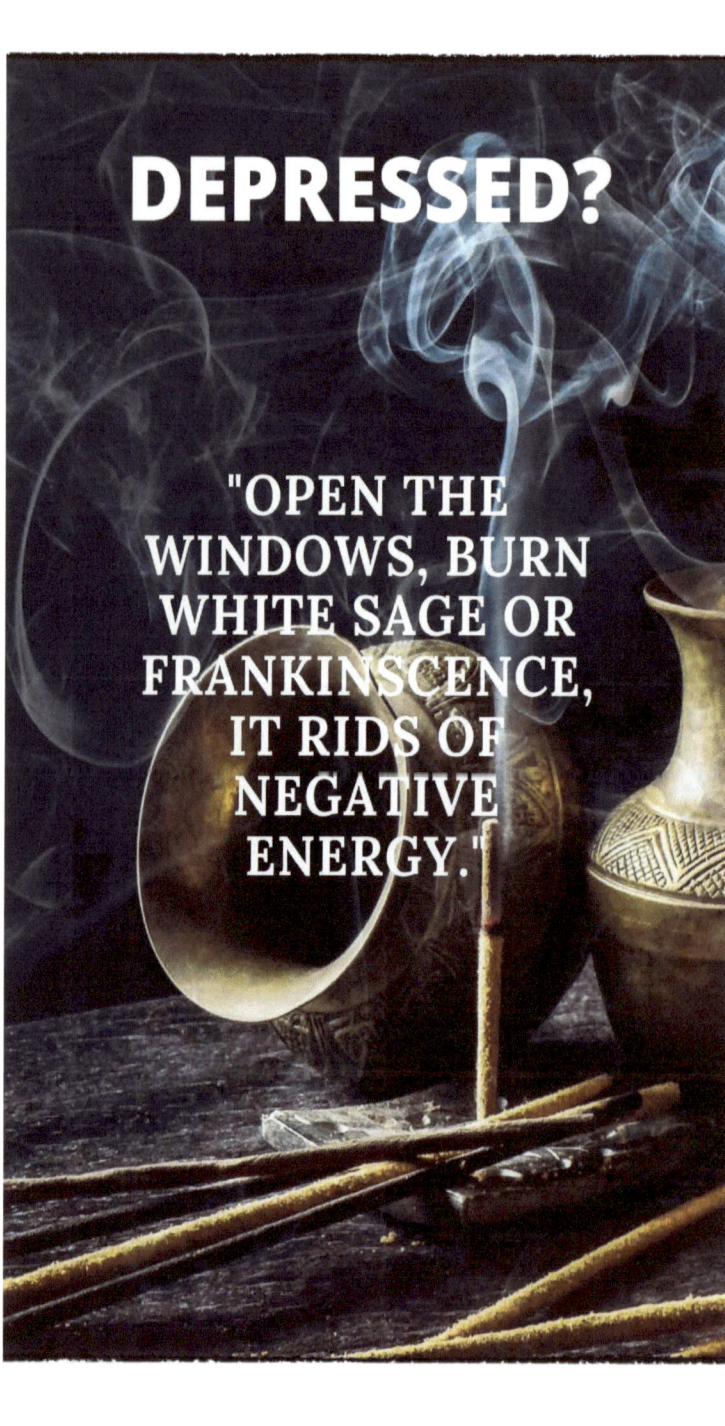

"Depression"

"Any external source of negative energy can cause you to feel depressed, angry or fearful. Energies are very easy to pick up from anyone or from anywhere. They can latch onto you when you've allowed yourself to be vulnerable. When we are feeling low, our vibrations are easy targets for negative forces. When we are happy, our vibrations are at a higher realm thereby making them an easy target for positive forces.

Here are some tools to use that are effective in cleansing negative energies in any space in which you dwell: White Sage or Frankincense Incense – open the windows when burned, it is utilized to rid a space of negative energies/spirits."

"Sleeplessness"

"Your bedroom should be a space of peace and relaxation before you enter a dream state of being. Music affects the soul. Soothing and instrumental relaxing music is key to creating a space of peace while sipping on chamomile tea and enjoying the fragrance of a lavender candle. Set the atmosphere and turn the TV off!"

"Overwhelmed"

"Nature is God and being amongst His beauty is healing. While walking in nature and being admired by the beauty, begin to inhale for 3 counts, exhale for 6 counts. Continue this until you feel relaxed and all thoughts in your mind are silent. Breathing deeply is necessary to operate fully and be in alignment with the Universe. Breathing brings forth oxygen to the brain. Oxygen is vital for brain healing and its proper function.

"Anxious"

Hyssop is a herb symbolized as a common cleansing in the Old Testament of the Bible- "Cleanse me with hyssop, and I will be clean" Psalm 51:7

Speak out-loud the entire 91st Psalm, it eliminates anxiousness.

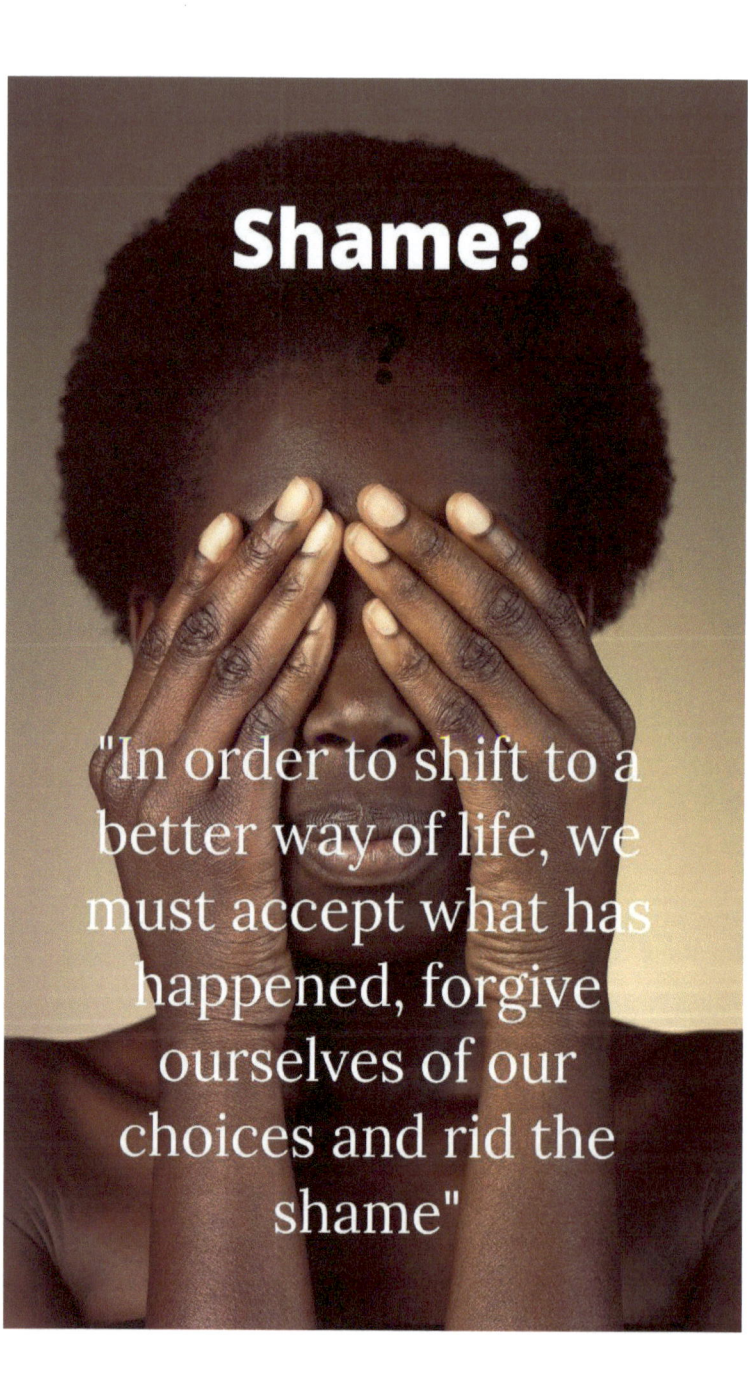

"Shame"

"How we were raised as a child plays a huge part in which path we choose to live our lives. Because of free will, we have the choice to create what type of life we desire. Some choices along the way have created us to live in bondage and shame. In order to shift to a better way of life, we must accept what has happened, forgive ourselves of our choices, rid ourselves of the shame and make a conscious decision not to return to that path and begin to make better decisions in life so that our children will become better than us."

Quotes to Remember

"The HOLY SPIRIT is recognized as a MAJOR tool to accomplish DESTINY!"

"Destiny is not a matter of chance, it's a matter of choice"

"If you can see an opportunity as quickly as you can see the faults of others, you will soon be rich."

"My opportunities will not go against my first priority as Mother."

"FAITH allows the mind to free itself from doubt, fear and discouragement.

"Discouragement is the shrewdest tool in the devil's tool kit."

"Aligning my MIND, BODY and SPIRIT will PRESERVE my TRUEST SELF."

The Creator has given us the right of absolute control over only one thing and that is our mind.

"My body with which nature has provided me will automatically maintain itself in perfect working order when I keep MY mind free from negative thoughts."

"The combination of Love and Sex is a power that steps up the vibration rate of every cell in the body for the perpetuation (to preserve from extinction) of life."

"One way of creating self-preservation comes through having children and living longevity by operating in my life's purpose, guided by the Almighty Divine Intelligence."

"Choosing life is everlasting."

"I will not allow life to push me around. God, the Holy Spirit and I PUSH life in the direction where

LOVE, JOY and PEACE dwell."

"Naps are essential to the subconscious mind."

"Human beings are balls of energy...our thoughts carry frequencies just like a radio/antenna."

"Telepathy is sometimes dangerous, as we pick up vibrations from other minds and often act upon them, imagining that they originated with ourselves.

To control such — surround yourself with like minds of greatness and purity."

"Without VISION my people perish…"

"Vision is produced by the subconscious mind. Vision allows me to FEEL the experience of my desires manifested…"

"VISION=PROPHETIC imagery when operating in the subconscious mind."

"Vision is manifested by letting go of what is in my present circumstances."

The definition of the Holy Spirit speaking: "Such an increase of the vibratory rate of the mind (electronically high frequency) enables you to tune in on a higher plane of communication that is not ordinarily experienced."

"REPLACE fear WITH faith. This changes the mindset of people from panic to achievement."

"How to connect with God? Observe, experiment, feel, pray, meditate and maintain positive thoughts.

"Applied Faith is the generator of electric power."

"Negative thinking creates ill health."

"The older I become, the more useful I am."

"Subconscious Mind= a fertile garden, Life's Purpose=seed."

"FEAR of Poverty results from failing to make your OWN decisions."

"Favor is when Opportunity MEETS Preparation."

"Blessed are the risk-takers for they bring us the future!"

"Opportunity attaches itself to the first person who recognizes it!"

"Being in need is not the same as being ready to receive."

"The thing that kept me going was the deep-seated conviction that the day would come when I not only would justify the many years put into this assignment but would be proud of myself for having stuck to the job until it was finished."

"FAITH in GOD is what allows endurance to manifest"

"The MIND is a blueprint of the physical manifestation. Be careful of your thoughts!"

"Imagination = create ideas and plans, Conscious = test moral justice, Memory=serves as keeper of records of experiences on a hard disk and finally

Inspiration= comes from the Divine."

"The TRUE origin of man's activity lies in his unceasing impulse to embody outside himself the DIVINE and SPIRITUAL elements within himself."

"Avoid naysayers, joy killers and pessimists."

"Great minds have purpose - others have wishes."

"Fear and Faith CANNOT occupy the same mind. One WILL dominate."

"Opportunity has a peculiar way of stalking the person who can recognize it and is ready to embrace it."

I pray with FAITH because I examine the existence of my Creator as it is provided by the order of the Universe.

"FEAR is the #1 cause of depriving opportunity."

"I have changed my WORLD around me to the COLOR of Hope and Faith because I have changed the ENTIRE tempo of vibration in my being."

Excerpts from "Healing Cosmetologist"

Copyright © 2015 Nicole Lee

Note: Napoleon Hill Foundation has consented to our use of all quotes throughout this book.

28 days of Prosperity by J. D. Bottroff

Today every person I meet has something to teach me about bringing forth my goal. I now release all doubt I have toward people.

Today I open the door to my good by choosing to forgive everyone I feel has wronged me. I now release negative feelings I have towards others.

Today I unlock the potential of my circumstance by knowing greater good is unfolding through every one of them. I release all fear of apparent adverse circumstances.

Today I choose to experience the peace of knowing that God is in charge of my goal. I release all doubt that God is in charge.

Today I experience the peace of knowing that God is guiding me through every step I take. I release all fear to act on my inner guidance.

Today I remind myself often that God and I are in Divine partnership. My success is assured. I release all negative feelings toward the success of my goal.

Today I feel the joy of knowing my goal is unfolding in Divine order. I now release all doubt that my life is unfolding as it should.

Today I am secure in knowing that God is in charge. I am relaxed and I am at peace. I release my belief that I am limited in any way.

Today I allow the peace of God to reign in my mind and heart. I am free to enjoy this day. I now release all apprehension about this day.

Today I choose to experience the comfort of knowing that my goal is unfolding in Divine order. I now release everything in my conscious and subconscious mind that blocks my good.

Today I live with awareness of God's guiding presence. Every step I take is the right step. I now release all fear that I can make a mistake.

Today I look beyond appearances and know that greater good is now unfolding in my life. I release all doubt that greater good is now unfolding in my life.

Today I experience the joy of knowing that my goal is already complete and is now manifesting. I release all doubt that my goal is manifesting.

Today I pause often to imagine myself experiencing the joy of my completed goal. I now release any concern about my goal.

Today I realize that everyone I meet is a channel through which God unfolds some aspect of my goal. I am open and receptive to the gifts everyone brings to my life. I release all negative attitudes toward people now.

Today I feel the peace of knowing that every action I take is a Divine action that leads me one step closer to my goal. I now release the belief that I am capable of taking wrong actions.

Today I am grateful that my goal is manifesting in Divine order. I am at peace.

Today I am grateful for all the many blessings this day brings. Something good is happening every moment. I now release all doubt that something good is happening now.

Today I am grateful for every person that comes into my life. They are a blessing to me, and I am a blessing to them. I now release all my distrust in people knowing that each is an instrument of God.

Today I am grateful for the prospering and attracting power of God's love, that which is rightfully mine is now brought into my life. I release all negative energy that repels my good.

Today I pay attention to all the blessings this day brings. I live each moment expecting the very best from God. I release all negative thoughts and feelings I have concerning the potential of this day.

CLOSING PRAYER:

I give thanks that the unlimited power of God continues to work mightily through me. My life is unfolding in Divine order and I am ready to take the next step.

Thoughts?

Words from the Author

My name is Nicole Lee- Warrior Mom of 3, Self-Published Author and Owner of The Doula of Entrepreneurship where my mission is to eradicate negative thinking through emotional well-being tools, entrepreneurial strategies, and empowerment. My goal is to positively impact relationships, nurture environments and build cultural interconnectedness.

"During my journey after the Divine God had me to become a fulltime mom, He led me to begin studies of the Napoleon Hill philosophies through a home study that Purdue

Calumet University offered. This was where I discovered a more defined meaning of what I had been practicing and experiencing; excerpts from my studies and notes are as follows:

-Positive energy creates positive thoughts and positive thoughts bring about high frequencies. By creating high frequencies, you will begin to draw positive results. Thoughts generate attitude and attitude influences thought.
-Keep your mind on the things you want and off the things you don't want. Thoughts affect every part of our being. They can produce emotional reactions that range from healthy to unhealthy.

Below are samples of how positive and negative thoughts create such emotions:

-Positive thoughts create positive outcomes by having a positive mental attitude, joy, happiness, enthusiasm, a calm spirit, a sense of well-being, achievement, ease, sense of fulfillment, extraordinary energy, a sense of worthiness, love, physical healing, emotional healing and an excitement about life.

-Positive thinking pays back major dividends.

-Negative thoughts creates negative outcomes by having negative attitudes: hate, unnecessary judging, tension, a sense of unworthiness, anxiety, mistrust, fatigue, embarrassment, illness, anger, resentment, depression, fear, alienation, or even catastrophic thinking – if the negative thinking is allowed to continue for too long a period.

The bottom line is negative thinking costs us mentally, physically, emotionally and spiritually.

"Trying to conquer that which you do not want is to live out a nightmare. Steadily moving toward the state of being you desire is an exciting adventure."

~Gary W. Edwards

- Spend less time in negative thinking. Contrary to what you may have learned earlier in life – please know, *it is* healthy to talk to yourself.

Tell yourself to *stop* when a negative thought enters your mind and then make a conscious effort to replace that thought with one that is positive. Avoid, when you can, those people who have what you do not want: a negative mental attitude.

Instead associate yourself with the most positive, caring people you can find."

~Excerpts from "Healing Cosmetologist"

Note: Napoleon Hill Foundation has consented of our use of all quotes throughout this book.

Publications:

- *Healing Cosmetologist*
- *Insight*
- *Warrior Survival Kit*
- *Emotional Remedies Calendar*
- *How to Eradicate Emotional Paralysis- Guide for Single Moms*
- *How to Write and Publish My Own Book*
- *Healing Beauty*
- *Wisdom of a Queen*
- *Don't Touch My Hair!*
- *How to Eradicate Fear- A Guide for Entrepreneurs*
- *Savagery, a Cinematic Therapeutic Production*
- *How to Eradicate Emotional Paralysis- A Guide for Everybody.*

Visit Nicole Online:

Website:
www.DoulaOfEntrepreneurship.com

LinkedIn: Nicole Lee and Healing in Cosmetology Group

www.ingramcontent.com/pod-product-compliance
Lightning Source LLC
Chambersburg PA
CBHW042337150426
43195CB00001B/26